Recycling

MAKE YOUR OWN
TOYS

The Five Mile Press Pty Ltd
950 Stud Road, Rowville
Victoria 3178 Australia
Email: publishing@fivemile.com.au
Website: www.fivemile.com.au

Published in 2006
Printed in China 5 4 3

Recycling Fun!

Make Your Own Toys

The Five Mile Press

Contents

1 Can Stilts

Soup and other food cans are very strong structures. With them we can make toys that support weight, like these metal stilts. It's a very old and simple idea. It's always fun walking on these painted cans because you have to move your feet along with the stilts and control your movements with the strings!

Tools and materials

1 Metal cans with a 10 cm diameter
2 Permanent marker
3 Scissors
4 Gimlet
5 Paint container
6 Ruler
7 Thick and fine paintbrushes
8 Thick string
9 Acrylic paint: red, black and blue

Can Stilts

1

When you have the can clean and ready, use a ruler to mark a line that divides the base of the cans into approximately two equal halves. To do this, take any point on the edge of the circular base and measure from this point to the most distant point on the opposite side of the base. In this case, it should measure about 10 cm. Using a permanent marker, mark the line that you have just measured.

2

When you have drawn the line to the other edge of the can, make a mark near this spot 2 cm below the base, as shown in the picture.

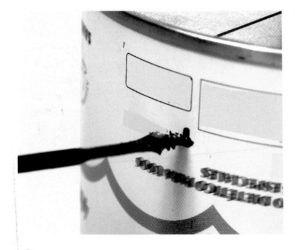

When poking the hole, the can must be standing in a vertical position, and you must hold the base of the can steady while drilling with the gimlet.

3

On the spot that you have just marked, poke a hole in the can. To do this, you will have to ask an adult to help you use the gimlet. When you poke the hole, do not press on the can too much, or else the metal will bend or become deformed.

4

Now, poke a hole in the opposite side of the can, at the other end of the horizontal line.

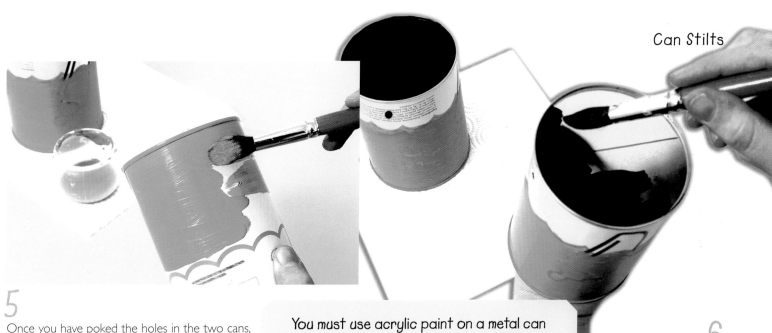

5

Once you have poked the holes in the two cans, you can paint them! Begin painting the side of the can. In this case, we will take advantage of the picture that is printed on the can, so that we can paint the sides in two different colours. If we follow the picture, we can see where we must paint with the blue paint, and from what point we will paint in red.

You must use acrylic paint on a metal can because it is the only paint that will stick to a non-porous material like metal. You must not mix the paint in a lot of water – the thicker the paint is, the better it will cover the metal.

6

Once you have painted the blue side of the can, you can begin painting the bottom of the can black while the blue paint is drying.

While you let the paint dry, measure off two 100 cm pieces of string.

When you have to measure off string or cardboard and the ruler is not long enough, take an in-between measurement like 50 cm and repeat it until it adds up to the right measurement. In this case, take the string and measure off 50 cm twice.

To cut the string you must use scissors. Make sure that you make a straight cut rather than a slanted cut. This way you will prevent the string from fraying.

Can Stilts

7 When the black and blue paint has dried, use a medium paintbrush to paint the top of the can, right above the blue paint. Be careful not to cross the paintbrush over into the area that you have already painted blue!

8 Once the cans are painted, they may look similar to the ones in the picture. In this case we did not paint the gold coloured rim or lip at the base of the can because we wanted to use the can's original colour. We have also painted a fun motif on each can.

9 Take the can in one hand and with the other hand insert the string, from the inside out, through one of the holes.

11 Once you have fed the string through one of the holes from the inside out, feed the same end of the string, which you have removed from the first opening, through the first hole, but in the opposite direction — from the outside in.

10 Insert the string through one of the holes, taking care not to fray it or snag it on the rough edges inside the can.

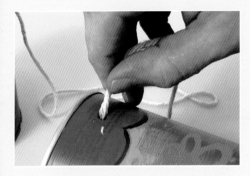

12

Insert your hand in the can. Take the string and pull a small section of it through the hole.

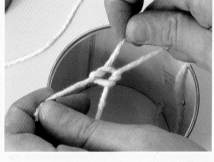

13

Take the two ends of the string inside the can and tie them in a double knot, so that the ends do not slip out of the can.

When you tie the knots, make sure that the two strings in both cans measure the same length, so that when you put the stilts on and you grab the string with your hands, they are at the same height.

14

Once you have tied the two ends in a knot, pull the string up, so that it stays taut inside the can. Done? Now you are ready to test-drive your stilts!

2 Marble Maze

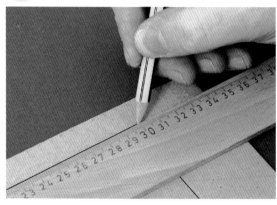

Some of the most useful and easily recyclable objects for making toys and crafts are cardboard boxes. Check the thickness of the cardboard before you begin, because it might be thin or more rigid depending on what type of box it is. In this exercise we will use two different thicknesses of cardboard – a rigid type for the base and a thinner one for the walls of the maze.

1

Take a thick cardboard box and cut a flat piece from one of the sides. Draw a line 30 cm long near the edge of the cardboard.

Tools and materials

1. Thin cardboard
2. Cutting pad
3. Stanley knife
4. Scissors
5. Pencil
6. Eraser
7. Glue
8. Thick cardboard
9. Thick permanent markers
10. Fine tip marker
11. Ruler

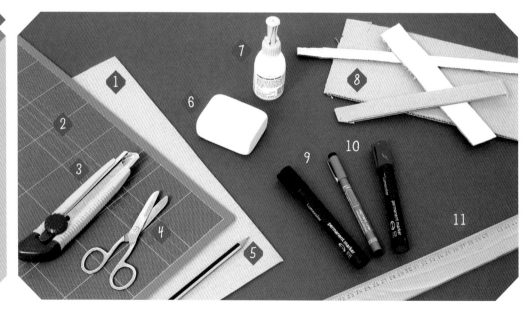

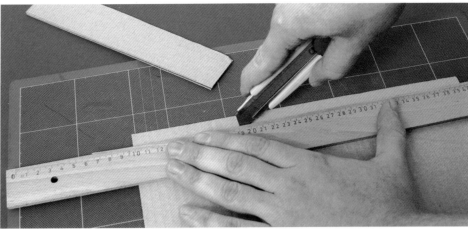

2

From each end of this line draw two more 20 cm lines – forming a 30 cm by 20 cm rectangle.

Ask an adult to help you use the stanley knife.

3

Over a cutting pad, cut a 30 cm by 20 cm rectangle with a stanley knife.

5

On the two 30 cm lines make marks every 2 cm, as shown in the picture.

4

To make a correct cut, you might have to go over the same line a couple of times with the stanley knife because the cardboard may be very thick.

6

On the 20 cm lines of the rectangle, also make marks every 2 cm, just like you did with the 30 cm lines.

Marble Maze

7

Now, using a pencil, connect the marks to form a grid in which each square measures 2 cm by 2 cm.

Use the pencil to mark out the sides of the grid, which will form the basis of your maze route. To make the route, you have to decide on a beginning and an end to the maze and design a correct path. It may help to think that each line that you draw will be a wall in the maze.

9

Erase the parts of the grid where you are not going to place any wall. The marks that you erase will form the route for the marble.

10

You can design the route however you want. Keep in mind that you can put up very long or very short walls, depending on whether you want the marble to have a straight route or a more winding one.

11

Using a fine tip marker, mark the lines of the grid that will be the walls. This way you will not confuse these marks with the pencil lines that you still have not gotten a chance to erase.

12

Now you can completely erase all the pencil marks in the maze design. You will be able to work better now that only the walls outlined in marker are visible.

13

Using a stanley knife, cut all of the wall sections that you have marked with a fine tip marker. Ask an adult to help you do this.

14

Next, take a sheet of thinner cardboard and on it draw a rectangle measuring approximately 10 cm by 20 cm.

To design the maze route, you must remember that the shorter the walls are, the more complicated the route will be. If the walls are longer, the marble will go faster – but the game will be simpler!

When you are marking the walls for the route, make sure that they never form a square or rectangle or any other closed form. This will make everything easier, as you will not have to work with any area that is totally cut out.

15

On the 10 cm sides of the rectangle that you have just made, mark lines every 1 cm. By doing this, you will be able to form 20 cm by 1 cm strips.

16

Using scissors or the stanley knife, cut the strips that you have just marked. Remember that if you work with a stanley knife, you must ask an adult for help, and you must always cut on a cutting surface.

Marble Maze

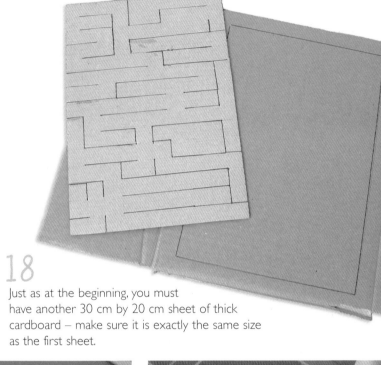

17
Now take the first sheet of cardboard and place it on a piece of thick cardboard to trace its shape.

18
Just as at the beginning, you must have another 30 cm by 20 cm sheet of thick cardboard – make sure it is exactly the same size as the first sheet.

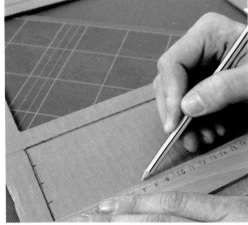

19
With a stanley knife and the help of an adult, cut out the sheet of cardboard that you have just traced.

20
On the same type of rigid cardboard that you have used for the two 30 cm by 20 cm sheets, draw a 30 cm by 8 cm rectangle.

21
On the 8 cm sides of the rectangle, make a mark every 2 cm, just as you have done before to make the 30 cm by 1 cm strips.

When you are cutting a piece from the cardboard box, don't use any of the folded parts of the cardboard box – the cardboard will not be rigid enough.

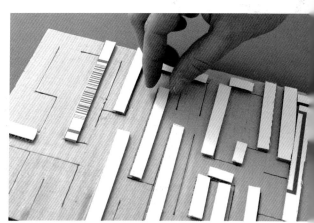

22

Connect the marks on both sides to make four 30 cm by 2 cm strips, as shown in the picture.

23

With the help of an adult, cut the strips that you have just drawn. To do this, use a stanley knife and work on a cutting surface.

24

Now go back to the design of the marble maze. Take one of the 1 cm by 30 cm strips that you have cut and mark on it the length of one of the walls drawn on the sheet of cardboard with the marble route. Look at the picture above and you will see how easy it is to mark the length of each wall in the route.

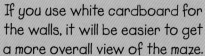

If you use white cardboard for the walls, it will be easier to get a more overall view of the maze.

26

Repeat the process of marking and cutting the pieces for the walls, one by one.

27

So that you don't make a mistake and have to later try to find which section of the route belongs to each wall, as you cut the wall place them on the board in the correct place.

25

Cut the strip of cardboard where you have marked the length of the wall. Use scissors and make sure that the cut is clean and straight.

Marble Maze

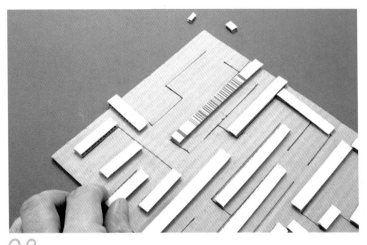

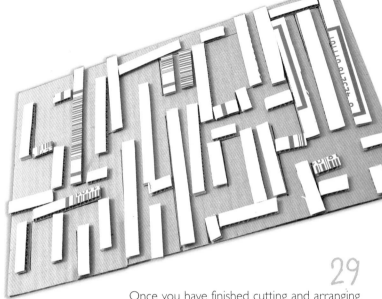

28

It would be a good idea for you to start placing the vertical walls first and, once they are in place, start placing the horizontal walls. This way, your work will be much more orderly. We also recommend that you begin cutting the long walls first and the shorter ones last.

29

Once you have finished cutting and arranging the walls of the route, the maze will look similar to the one in the picture. It may be that when you have marked the route with the marker, you have marked a wall that you no longer want in the maze. You can eliminate it easily by just cutting off the piece of wall that you do not want.

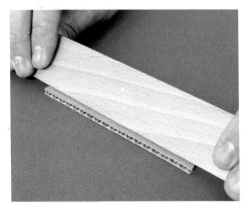

31

You must make sure that one side of the walls is flattened, to make it easier to insert into the slots on the base.

30

Once you have arranged all of the walls, take each one by their end, and using the edge of the ruler, flatten the part of the wall that you will insert in the cardboard base that you have cut at the beginning with the stanley knife.

32

Look at the picture above to see how the wall should look once you have flattened one of its sides. You will see that it has a wedge shape, so that it is easier to place it in the right spot.

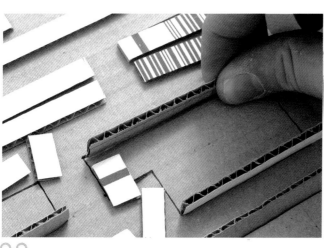

33

As you are flattening each one of the walls, return them to their spots on the board and place them in the appropriate slot. This way the cardboard walls will take on the right shape.

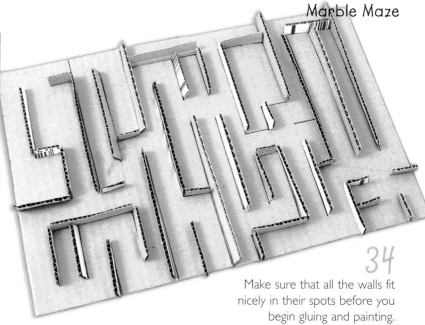

34

Make sure that all the walls fit nicely in their spots before you begin gluing and painting.

35

Remove the walls from the cardboard one by one and paint them with a thick permanent marker. If your markers have a flat tip, it will be easier to paint large surfaces like these.

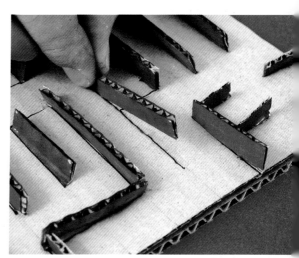

36

You can also paint the top of the cardboard wall. This way, although you will not completely hide the spaces in the ribbed cardboard, at least you will cover them up a bit.

37

Paste a little glue in the slot where you are going to place a piece of wall. Do not press down on the cardboard because, when you insert the cardboard wall, it might squash the glue down the slot.

Marble Maze

38
While the glue on the maze walls is drying, you can begin painting the 2 cm by 30 cm strips that you have cut before. Paint them on both sides and on the top, just as you have done with the red walls. This time, use a black marker.

39
Mark the beginning and the end of the maze with a marker. To do this, simply mark an arrow on one of the corners and a cross on the opposite corner to symbolise the start and finish lines.

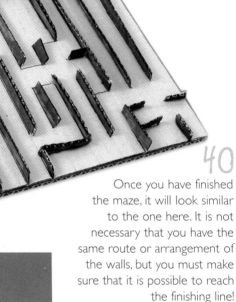

40
Once you have finished the maze, it will look similar to the one here. It is not necessary that you have the same route or arrangement of the walls, but you must make sure that it is possible to reach the finishing line!

41
Take the second sheet of cardboard that you have cut, and spread glue on it.

42
Very carefully, stick the maze onto the cardboard sheet that you have just pasted. This way you will make the entire structure more stable.

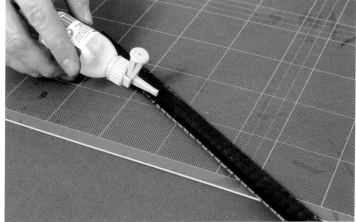

43

Taking care not to ruin the walls, press down on the edges of the two sheets of cardboard to make sure that the two pieces stick together nicely.

When you want to paste a very large surface, you must spread the glue evenly over the entire surface.

44

To finish, paste glue on one of the cardboard strips that you have painted black. You must put glue on the bottom of one of the long sides of the strip, as shown in the picture.

45

Stick the strip to one of the sides of the two cardboard sheets. Do not press very hard or else you will ruin the walls of the maze.

46

Repeat this process with another black strip and stick it opposite the one that you have just placed. Finally, glue both the short strips onto the short sides of the maze.

Marble Maze

When you stick the black strips on the short sides, you will see that part of the black cardboard sticks out from the short sides of the maze board. Cut these overhanging parts off carefully, so that the strips do not come unglued.

Once you have finished the maze, choose your favourite marbles, (they can't be too big!) and start playing with them. You can move the maze with your hands and try to make the marble travel the shortest route.

3 Articulated Snake

The cardboard tubes that are normally found in rolls of toilet paper or paper towels are very useful for creating animal shapes. They can be used to make the body, the legs, or even the head of the animal, without having to bend the cardboard into a cylinder shape, which is very difficult to do. This exercise will combine the structure of the cardboard tubes with a paper fastener hook system that will allow us to give the snake points of articulation or joints.

Tools and materials

1. Hole puncher
2. Glue stick
3. Thick yellow, black and red markers
4. Ruler
5. Thin cardboard – yellow, light-green and dark-green
6. Thick marker
7. Pencil
8. Washers for the metal fasteners
9. Scissors
10. Cutting pad
11. Metal paper fasteners
12. Adhesive tape
13. Cardboard tubes from rolls of paper towels
14. Stanley knife
15. Egg carton

Articulated Snake

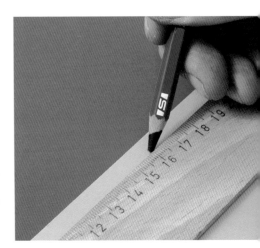

2

On each thin piece of cardboard, make two marks at a distance of 16 cm from the bottom edge.

1

Take three cardboard tubes from three rolls of paper towels and cut the tubes in half. For this exercise you could also use tubes from rolls of toilet paper, although the cardboard from the rolls of paper towels is better because it is made of a softer cardboard. The cut needs to be made with a stanley knife, so you will have to ask an adult for help.

Cut the cardboard tubes in the middle. You can choose to make some longer and some shorter sections, but you must then change the dimensions of the thin cardboard squares.

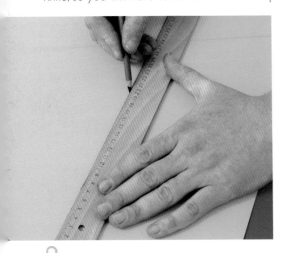

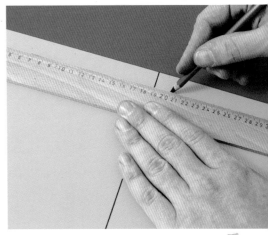

3

Connect both marks by drawing a horizontal line across the entire thin cardboard, as shown in the picture.

4

Make marks every 16 cm on this line, starting from one end.

5

Repeat this process on the bottom edge of the thin cardboard and connect the marks on the horizontal line and on the bottom edge to make three 16 cm by 16 cm squares.

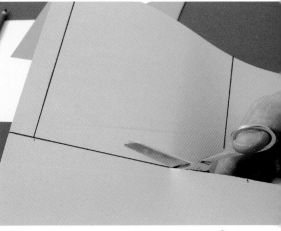

6
Repeat the same process on all of the thin pieces of cardboard – yellow, dark-green and light-green cardboards.

7
Using scissors, cut out the area where the squares are drawn. You should get three squares of each colour.

8
When you have cut out all the pieces of thin cardboard, paste glue over each of the six sections of cardboard tubes that you cut at the beginning.

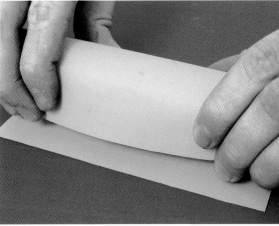

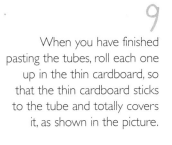

9
When you have finished pasting the tubes, roll each one up in the thin cardboard, so that the thin cardboard sticks to the tube and totally covers it, as shown in the picture.

10
When you finish wrapping the thin cardboard around each tube, just check that it covers each one completely. If necessary, use a little adhesive tape to make the end of the thin cardboard stick nicely.

Articulated Snake

11

Repeat this process with all of the cardboard tubes. Alternate the colours, so that for each colour you get two tubes.

12

Cut the thin cardboard hanging over the edges of the tubes so that they form a point or wedged shape. To do this, cut two triangles on each end of the covered tubes, one on each side, as shown in the picture.

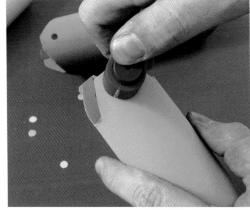

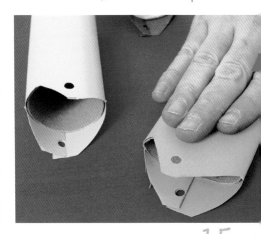

13

When you cut the thin cardboard, do not cut the cardboard tube on the inside. Observe the picture. You can see that the cardboard tube is not cut, but rather, a cut is made right up to its edge.

14

On each overhang of thin cardboard, you will have to make a hole. Take the hole puncher and punch a hole in the middle of each of the overhanging ends on each side of the tube.

15

Once you have punched a hole in all of the sections, flatten them with your hand to make the tubes look more like a snake. Snakes do not have a round body. Rather, they are slightly flat so their bodies rest on their bellies.

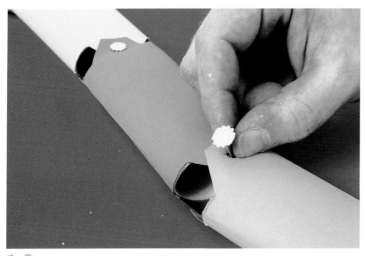

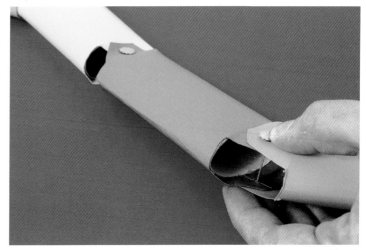

16

Connect the sections of the tubes by overlapping the thin cardboard that is overhanging the tubes, as shown in the picture. Match up the holes of each overhang and insert a metal paper fastener through the opening.

17

The paper fastener must go completely through the tubes and come out at the bottom opening where you have also matched up the holes.

The overhangs do not need to be a certain size or perfectly symmetrical because the movement of the snake will hide any possible defects in these areas.

Overlap the pieces of thin cardboard and make sure that the part that is on top is always the same, so that the form of the snake appears more continuous.

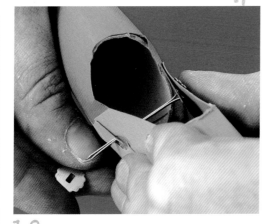

18

Carefully place the washer on the other side of the paper fastener at the bottom of the tube.

19

Making sure not to crush the cardboard tube or thin cardboard too much, open the paper fastener to secure the washer tightly against the thin cardboard – see below.

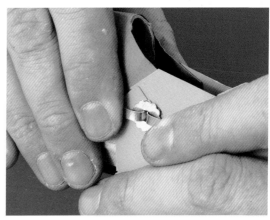

Articulated Snake

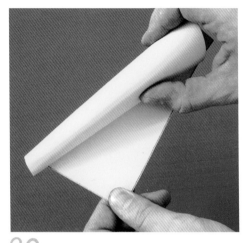

20
To make the tail of the snake, take the yellow square that is left over and roll it into a cone.

21
Use a glue stick to paste a little glue on the end of the thin cardboard, so that it sticks.

If you make the holes for the tail at different depths, this will raise the tail upward when you hook it on. You can also raise the tail by folding the area up a little where you will hook on the tail.

22
Once the glue is dry, use the paper puncher to punch two holes at the top and bottom of the snake's tail.

23
Match up the holes that you have just made with the holes in the last section of the covered cardboard tube. Insert the paper fastener to secure the tail to the snake.

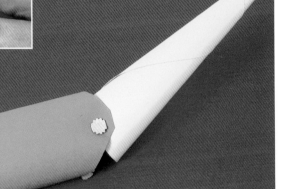

24
To make the snake's head, take an egg carton and cut off the part that would normally hold one egg. Place it in the end of a small piece of cardboard tube, as shown in the picture.

25

Look at the picture to see how the piece of egg carton fits inside the tube.

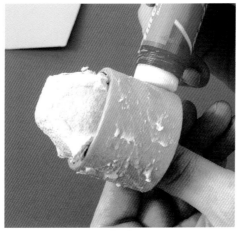

26

Use a glue stick to cover the cardboard tube area with a lot of glue, and stick a thin light-green piece of cardboard on it, in just the same way as you did before.

27

Cut two pointed wedge shapes in the back of the thin cardboard, so that you can hook it onto the body of the snake. Here you can see that we've left a lot of thin cardboard hanging over the end of the tube. By doing this, the head becomes more articulated than the body, which means it will be able to turn better.

28

At the tips of the wedges you have cut, punch two identical holes – one on the top and one on the bottom.

If necessary, you can secure the areas that you have glued with a little adhesive tape. This will make the cardboard stick better and the trick won't show because it will be on the bottom of the snake!

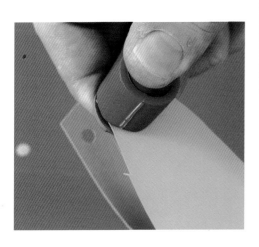

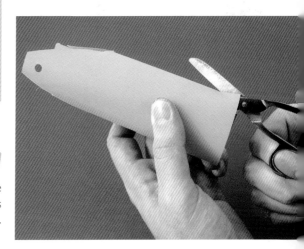

29

Make a cut in each side of the front of the snake's head as shown in the picture.

Articulated Snake

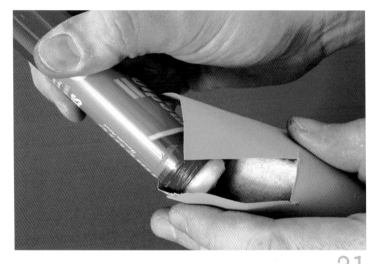

30

Using the cut that you have just made cut a triangle the other way around, with the wide part of the triangle touching the inner cardboard structure. You can see that the thin cardboard, when it is cut, takes on a bell shape.

31

Paste glue on the inside of the thin cardboard. Paste a lot of glue on the bottom especially.

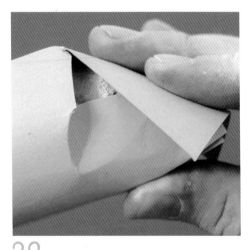

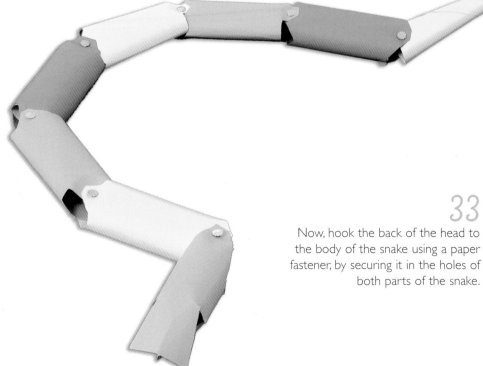

32

Fold in the bottom part of the thin cardboard and cover it with the top part, as shown in the picture.

33

Now, hook the back of the head to the body of the snake using a paper fastener, by securing it in the holes of both parts of the snake.

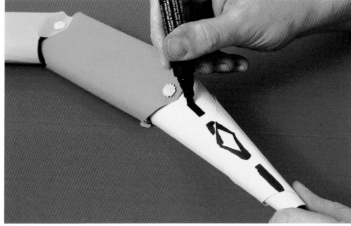

Snakes are usually covered with rhombuses and stripes that you can easily imitate with thick permanent markers.

34

When you have put the snake together, you can begin to decorate it. Because you have used coloured thin cardboard, you will save yourself from having to paint the entire snake. So, using permanent markers, draw in the stripes and geometric forms characteristic of snakes.

35

Using a black marker draw the eyes, and draw holes for the nose on the snake's head.

36

A snake's skin usually has geometric shapes like the diamond-shaped rhombus, which stretch all over its skin. Draw a rhombus in the centre of each one of the tube pieces. For the darker pieces of thin cardboard, use the yellow marker, and for the lighter pieces, use the black marker.

Articulated Snake

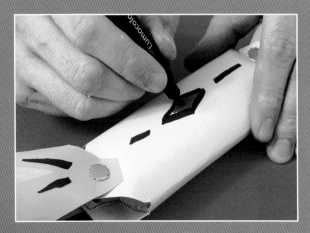

37
Paint the inside of the rhombuses and draw some lines around them to complete the decoration of the snake's skin.

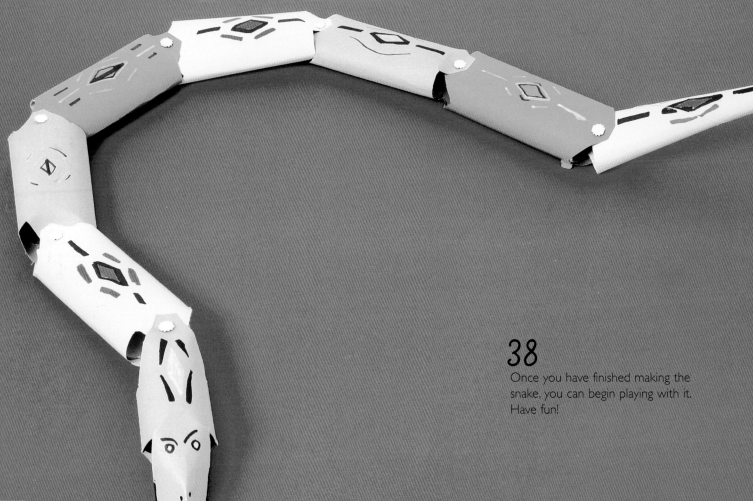

38
Once you have finished making the snake, you can begin playing with it. Have fun!

4 Polyester Aeroplane

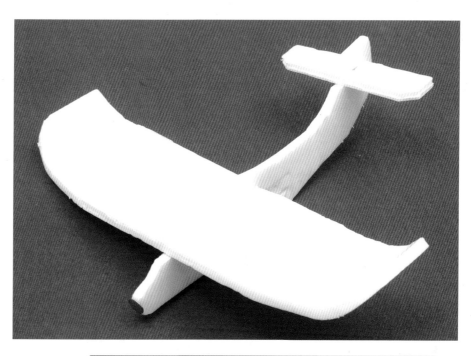

Expanded polyester (Porex) is a material that comes from petroleum that is manufactured through an industrial process which involves CFC gases. CFCs are chlorofluorocarbon gases and are directly responsible for the depletion of the ozone layer which protects us from solar radiation and shields our atmosphere. Therefore it is important that these types of containers (which are now beginning to be manufactured with less harmful processes) be reused at home – both to store food in the refrigerator and to make toys like these aeroplanes!

Tools
and materials

1. Porex tray
2. Paper
3. Thumbtacks
4. Stanley knife
5. Scissors
6. Pencil
7. Acrylic paint or several coloured permanent markers

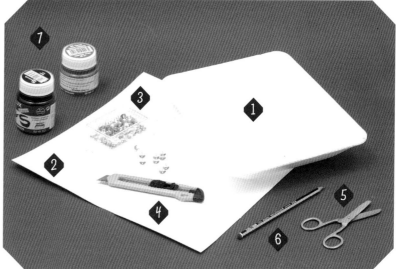

Polyester Aeroplane

The Porex tray that we are going to use is the sort that is used in supermarkets to package vegetables and meat.

1

First, draw the shapes of the aeroplane on paper. Since it is a very simple aeroplane, you only have to draw the shape of the wings, the body, and the ailerons at the tail. Very carefully cut the shapes out using scissors. Then, you can use a pencil to trace around the shapes on the Porex tray.

2

Using scissors, cut the Porex tray along the lines that you have just drawn.

3

If you need help to cut the Porex, ask an adult to cut the tray with a stanley knife. If you want, you can use the sides of the tray to raise the tips of the wings a little.

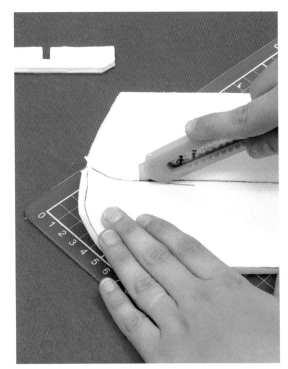

4

Once you have cut out the three pieces, make some notches to fit them together. To do this, you must find the midpoint of the piece that forms the wings. Halfway into it, cut a rectangle that is as thick as the piece of Porex that forms the body of the aeroplane. Repeat this process with the other pieces, making two notches in the middle of the aeroplane, one on the wings and another one on the ailerons at the tail.

The Porex tray can be cut with scissors or a stanley knife, but if you need help, ask an adult!

5

Mount the three pieces together using their notches, being careful not to break any piece. Start by mounting the ailerons at the tail.

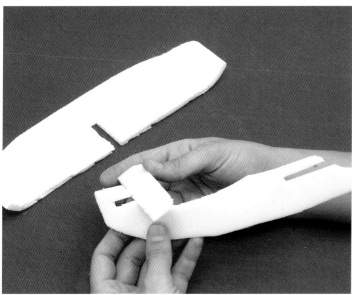

6

Next, mount the wings of the aeroplane. You must be careful with the areas around the notches because they are much more fragile than the rest of the plane.

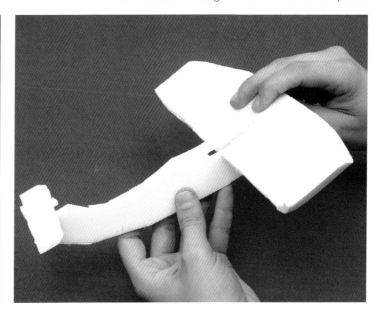

Polyester Aeroplane

7

Once you have mounted the pieces together, place a thumbtack in the nose of the aeroplane, so that it acts as a counterweight.

8

If you want, you can paint the aeroplane. Use acrylic paint if you want to paint the entire aeroplane. If you are only going to draw some decorations or insignias, you can use different coloured permanent markers. Now get ready for take-off!

5 A Fun Crocodile

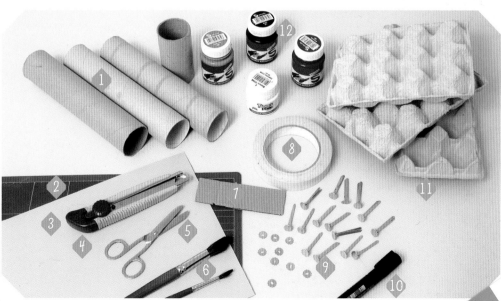

Y ou can make so many different things out of an egg carton. The cardboard used to make egg cartons is different from the cardboard used to make cardboard boxes. Because it is softer and more porous, you will be able to work with it rather effortlessly. To join the pieces you can use metal paper fasteners, and because it is such a soft cardboard, you will be able to punch holes in it using just your hands, and you will be able to work with all the pieces better.

1

Take one of the egg cartons and cut it into two pieces – one piece with 4 egg slots and another with 6 egg slots. Egg cartons can come with 12, 10 or 6 egg slots. Here we are using a carton with 10 slots, so when we cut it, we will have one piece with 3 x 2 slots and another with 2 x 2 slots.

Tools and materials

1. Cardboard tubes
2. Cutting pad
3. Thin cardboard
4. Stanley knife
5. Scissors
6. Paintbrushes
7. Little piece of cardboard
8. Adhesive tape
9. Metal paper fasteners
10. Black permanent marker
11. Different sized egg cartons
12. Red, green, black and white acrylic paint

A Fun Crocodile

2

Place one of the pieces that you have just cut on top of the other, as shown in the picture. Fit the pieces together using two paper fasteners to connect the pieces at the middle of the cartons.

3

Once you have connected both pieces together with the paper fasteners, the fasteners will allow the two pieces to open and close as shown in the picture. This will be the mouth of your crocodile!

5

Using a marker, mark two connecting spots in the place where the pieces of cardboard hook together. You will place paper fasteners in these spots.

4

Hook an egg carton with 12 slots to the back of the piece that you have just assembled. Make sure that you hook the piece for the crocodile's mouth to the middle of this egg carton.

6

Pressing down with your hands, place the two paper fasteners in the spots that you have marked. This cardboard is very soft so it will be easy for you to punch a hole in it with just the paper fastener.

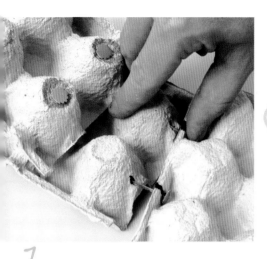

7

Hook both pieces together and make sure that the paper fasteners perfectly puncture the two pieces of egg carton.

6

As you move ahead in this exercise, check how your crocodile is coming along. Observe the pictures and make sure the crocodile is correct before you begin painting.

8

Once you have hooked the two pieces together, they must look the same as in the picture. Don't open the bottom of the paper fasteners yet because you will have to paint all of the pieces later.

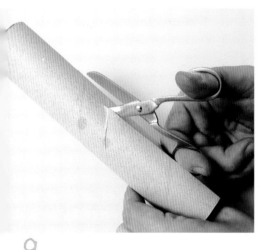

9

Take one of the cardboard tubes and cut it in half lengthways.

10

Once the tubes are cut, the two pieces must be flat, as in the picture. It is important that they are stable and stand steady on the ground because they will be the legs of your crocodile.

37

A Fun Crocodile

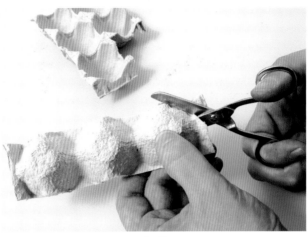

11

At the top of the egg carton place paper fasteners on two alternating slots in order to secure the cardboard tubes on the other side of the egg carton.

12

From another egg carton, cut a piece that is three or four slots long. At the last slot, cut the overhanging part of the carton into a pointed-shape.

Some egg cartons are smoother than others. To make this crocodile, the ideal carton should be rough and, if possible, yellow. This way, it will look more like the skin of a crocodile.

13

Hook this last piece of the carton to the middle slot of the egg carton. The one piece of egg carton must fit into the other perfectly, so that you can nicely mount what will be the tail.

14

You have now put the entire crocodile together. Make sure that the fasteners are centered in the right position. Now think about how you will paint each part of the crocodile!

15

Begin painting the middle part and the tail of the crocodile. To do this, use green acrylic paint and a thick paintbrush. Instead of applying long brushstrokes, it will be better to randomly tap the paintbrush on the egg carton. This way a little yellow will still show, which will give the appearance of the crocodile's scales.

16

Now paint the top of the crocodile's mouth in the same way and with the same green colour. Paint all of this part, because the eyes of the crocodile will be on the bottom.

17

Finally, paint the bottom of the crocodile green. It is not necessary that you paint the middle part, but do paint the pieces that show on the outside.

18

Now paint the part for the mouth. First paint the middle area bright red, since it will be the inside of the fierce crocodile's mouth.

19

Paint the outer part of the mouth white. This will make the crocodile look like it has teeth.

20

You have to paint the top and bottom of the mouth the same, taking into account where they will be. The teeth on the upper half will look fiercer because the egg carton has a broken shape that is similar to the shape of teeth in a mouth.

21

On the bottom of the crocodile's head you must paint two of the slots with a little white paint to make the eyes of the crocodile.

22

Paint both the top and bottom red and white to cover the colour of the egg carton completely.

24

Using black paint, completely cover the ends of the cardboard. Use undiluted paint to make sure that the original colour of the cardboard does not show through.

23

Paint the two halves of the cardboard tube using black acrylic paint. You will not need to cover them completely. Rather, you can leave the middle of the tube unpainted, so that you can hold it better.

25

To obtain a nice result, paint the long part of the cardboard tube in thick, wide brushstrokes.

26

When the white paint of the eyes has dried, paint a thin black line around the shape of the eyes. This will make the eyes of the crocodile more defined.

27

In the middle of the eye, paint a big black dot.

28

Alternatively, you can use a thick black permanent marker to apply a black dot in the middle of the white circles.

A Fun Crocodile

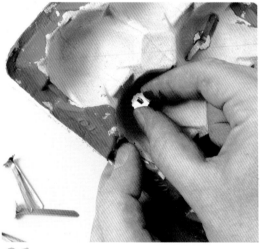

29

Place a piece of regular cardboard in the middle of the mouth, so that it stays open when you are mounting the paper fasteners.

30

Begin inserting the paper fasteners just as you did at the beginning of the exercise. Use the holes that you made then.

If you want, you can paint the gold head of the paper fasteners black, using a black permanent marker or by applying a drop of paint. However, the gold colour of the unpainted paper fasteners will not look bad because it will still match the colours you have painted the crocodile.

31

At the bottom of the crocodile, place the washers on the paper fasteners, as shown in the picture.

32

Once you have finished putting the mouth together, make sure that you have correctly painted all of the parts of the crocodile's head.

Acrylic paint is totally harmless. But it is a paint that gives off a rather strong odour, so it is advisable that you work with it in a well-ventilated place and that you let it dry outside.

33

Starting at the head and ending at the tail, secure all of the parts of the crocodile with paper fasteners. Attach the washers, making sure not to force the materials too much.

34

Once the crocodile is dry, you can put it in your room to keep people out, or you can simply play with it – perhaps making believe that you are on a safari on the Amazon or Nile Rivers!

6 Little Floating Boats

When you want to make a toy, the most important thing is that it works – if you make a car, it must be able to run and if you make a boat, it must float. This is why Porex is the perfect material to create these boats from, because it is a very light type of synthetic cork that you will be able to work with very easily. You will be able to paint it with bright colours and make these little boats float.

1

Draw a 7 cm line on a piece of paper. Next, draw a 7 cm by 4.5 cm rectangle using this line.

Tools and materials

1 Acrylic paint
2 Glue
3 Hole puncher
4 Cutting pad
5 Scissors
6 Ruler
7 Stanley knife
8 Plastic straws
9 Eraser
10 Paintbrush
11 Adhesive tape
12 Pencil
13 Black permanent marker
14 Thin light-coloured cardboard
15 Porex trays

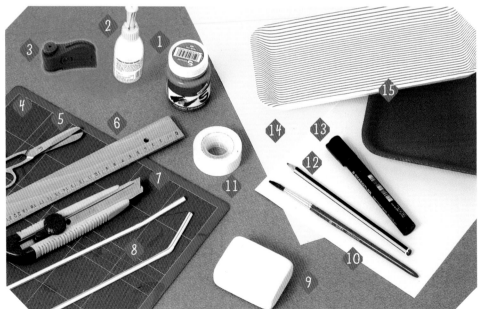

scheme

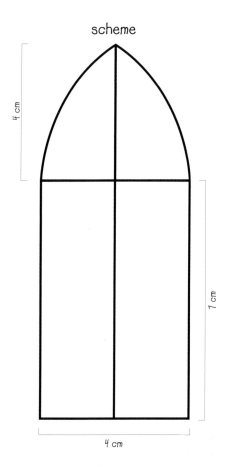

4 cm

7 cm

4 cm

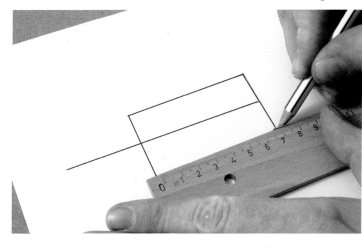

2 Divide the rectangle you have just drawn with a line in the middle that juts out on one of the sides.

3 Take the middle line that you have just drawn and extend it 4 cm outside of the rectangle.

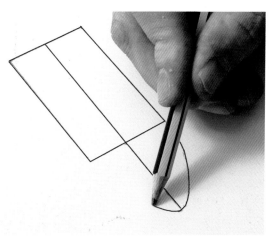

4 Draw two curved lines that connect the two long sides of the rectangle with the end of the middle line – at a distance of 4 cm from the rectangle.

To draw the curved lines there is a type of ruler that is called a French curve, which is made up of several different shaped curves that can help you. However, if you try to do it by hand, you will see that is not so difficult.

Little Floating Boats

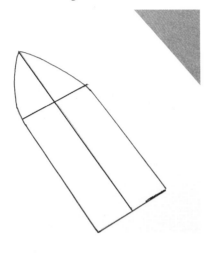

6

Take the scissors and cut out the silhouette of the boat that you have just drawn. It is advisable that you make a rather clean cut, so that you can use the pattern several times.

5

Once you have drawn all of the lines, you will have the silhouette of a simple boat. Look at the pattern if you need to make measurements.

When you make crafts, keep the patterns so that you can repeat the designs that you like the most. Once you have cut the paper, you will have the boat pattern forever!

7

Trace the shape of the boat on one of the Porex trays. Press down firmly with your pencil so the design is clear and visible.

8

Ask an adult for help using the stanley knife to cut the silhouette of the boat out of the Porex tray. It is very difficult to cut this material, so the stanley knife will have to go over the silhouette several times to cut it properly.

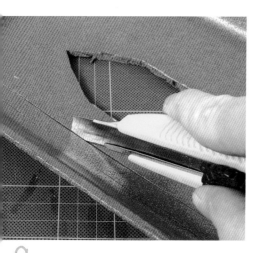

9

Cut two or three 2 cm wide strips from the Porex tray. To do this, ask an adult for help using the stanley knife to cut these strips out.

10

With these pieces that you have cut, you will have all the materials necessary for building your first boat!

12

Starting on the bottom of the boat, stick one of the 2 cm wide Porex strips that you have prepared.

11

Paste glue on the edge of the silhouette of the Porex boat. Do not worry if you notice that the Porex is poorly cut – it's a difficult material to cut and it won't affect the final outcome.

13

When you get to the curved part, continue sticking and pressing down with your hand, so that the Porex strip moulds to the shape of the boat.

Little Floating Boats

14

Using scissors, cut the overhanging part of the Porex strip that you have just stuck on. Make sure that you make a sharp and quick cut, so that you do not ruin the part that is stuck to the boat.

Porex is a material that sticks nicely and is easy to work with. You should easily be able to give it the curved shape that you will need to stick it on the front of the boat.

16

Cut the part of the Porex strip that overhangs, making sure that it covers the front of the boat neatly, as shown in the picture.

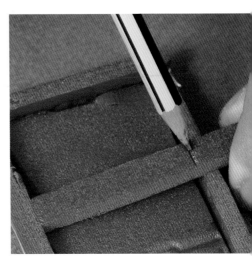

15

Stick the next Porex strip on the other side of the boat. Just like the first Porex strip, this strip will overhang a little, and you will have to cut it off.

17

On the back of the boat stick a piece of a Porex strip that has the same length as the width of the boat.

18

Take the third Porex strip that you have cut and place it on the boat, so that you can mark the width of the boat on the strip. Using a pencil, mark the spot along where you will have to cut the Porex strip.

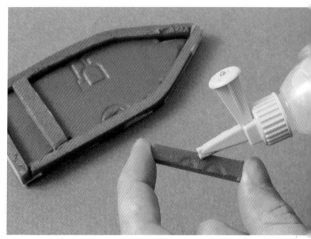

19
Cut the Porex strip along the mark that you have just made.

20
Repeat this exact same process for the front of the boat. You might not be able to use the same measurements, so you will have to mark the width of the boat again on the Porex strip.

21
Paste a little glue on both strips and stick them on the correct part of the boat. You can use two or three strips for the inside of the boat, whichever you prefer, since this will not affect its ability to float.

Acrylic paint is waterproof, so it is ideal for painting your aquatic crafts.

23
Start painting the top of the boat with green acrylic paint. If you want, you can leave the inside of the boat the original colour of the Porex.

24
Carefully paint the side of the boat using long and fluid brushstrokes and quite a lot of paint.

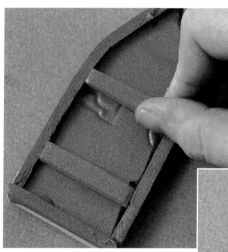

22
Press down well on the Porex strips that you are going to stick on, so that the glue adheres nicely. Glue takes a little while to dry on Porex.

Little Floating Boats

25
Let the boat dry on a sheet of paper and get ready to make the second boat, which, although it looks similar, will be a sailboat.

26
Using a pencil, trace the silhouette again, on another Porex tray.

27
In this picture, the Porex tray has stripes that you can use to better guide your pencil when tracing and marking the silhouette of the boat.

28
Cut the silhouette out of the Porex tray. If you want, you can use scissors, although it might be a little more difficult than using a stanley knife.

29
Repeat the same process of cutting and sticking the 2 cm wide Porex strips on the boat and stick them on, starting from the back of the boat and giving them the correct curved shape at the front of the boat.

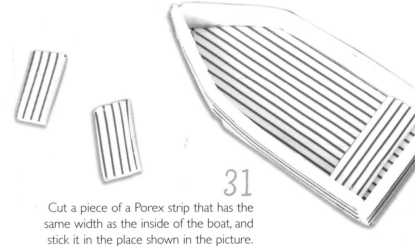

30
Use adhesive tape to secure the strips to the bottom of the boat.

31
Cut a piece of a Porex strip that has the same width as the inside of the boat, and stick it in the place shown in the picture.

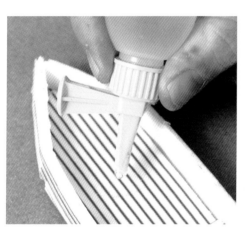

32
Paste a little glue on the middle of the boat, so that on this glued spot you can stick the two pieces of Porex that will act as the base for the sail.

33
Stick two pieces of Porex in the middle of the boat. They must be the same width as the inside of the boat, and the two pieces must be the same size.

34
Take a plastic straw and cut it, so that it is the same length as the boat. To do this, simply place the straw on the boat and cut off the part that overhangs.

Little Floating Boats

35

Using a pencil, punch a hole in the two pieces of Porex that you have stuck in the middle of the boat. In this hole you will insert the straw that will act as the mast for the sail.

36

Insert the straw in the hole that you have just punched in the Porex. Make sure that you insert it deep enough, so that it can bear the weight of the sail.

37

You can now begin painting the boat with undiluted green acrylic paint. Using this paint, the light colour of the Porex will not show through.

38

Once you have painted the entire boat, let it dry on a sheet of paper just as you did with the first boat that you built.

If you cannot correctly insert the straw in the hole, you can pinch the bottom of it to reduce its diameter.

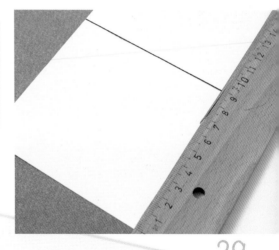

39

On a thin piece of yellow cardboard, draw a 9 cm by 9 cm square. Use one of the corners of the thin cardboard, so that it is easier to cut the square out.

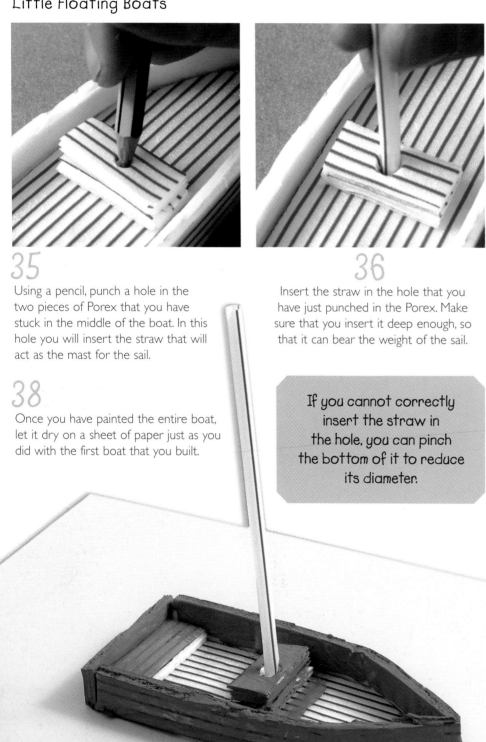

40

Using scissors, cut out the square that you have just drawn. Make sure that you make a clean cut because you will not be painting the sail and it will look just as you have cut it.

41

Draw a line on the piece of thin yellow cardboard that exactly divides the sail in half. Press down lightly with the pencil when marking this line.

42

At the two ends of the line that you have drawn down the middle of the thin cardboard, punch two holes using a paper puncher, as shown in the picture.

45

Once you have put the sail in place, it will look a little arched and it will stay attached to the upper part of the mast by its own pressure.

44

Next, insert the straw through the other hole at the top of the sail. The thin cardboard must look a little arched, as shown in the picture.

43

Insert the straw through one of the holes in the sail. Make sure that the line you have drawn in pencil is on the inside.

Little Floating Boats

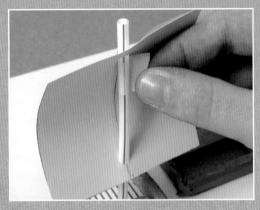

46
Put a little adhesive tape on the straw right beneath the top hole on the sail. This way you will prevent the thin yellow cardboard from sliding down the straw.

47
Put a little adhesive tape on the top end of the straw. Make sure that the tape sticks nicely and fold it in half. This way you will have a flag at the top of your sailboat's mast.

48
Once you have finished and the paint is totally dry, you will be able to sail your two Porex boats!

1 Locomotive

Home product containers are designed using basic geometric shapes. Cubes and cylinders can be combined to create more complex objects. If you really think about it, trucks, trains and planes are also made up of these shapes. A truck is simply a box with wheels, and a plane is a cylinder with wings.

In this exercise we are going to build an old-fashioned locomotive entirely out of containers that we find. It is very simple to build. You just need to think about which containers will be the right shape to make up the different parts of the locomotive!

Tools and materials

1 Tetra Brick carton
2 Cylindrical water bottle made from PET plastic
3 Small, thin cardboard box
4 Lids from jars of jam or vegetables.
5 Rectangular bottle made from PET plastic
6 Lids from water bottles.
7 Soft drink bottle made from PET plastic
8 Paper fasteners
9 Adhesive tape
10 White glue
11 Wooden ice-cream sticks
12 Acrylic paint: red, green and black
13 Permanent markers: gold, black and red.
14 Scissors
15 Stanley knife
16 Gimlet

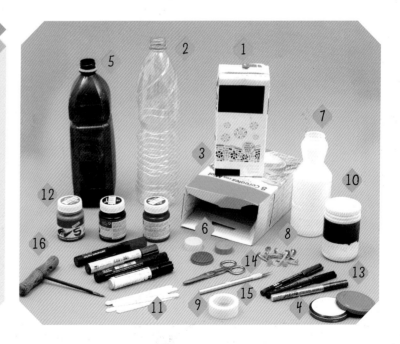

Locomotive

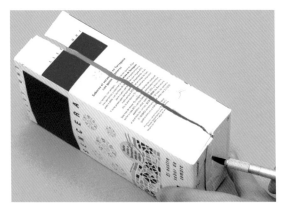

1

Using the stanley knife, cut the Tetra Brick in half so that you obtain a thin rectangular shape that will have an open bottom. This will mean you will be able to mount the paper fasteners from the bottom.

Before you use the containers, clean them off with water and dry them thoroughly with a paper towel.

2

Cut the cylindrical water bottle in half at its straightest part. To do this, you must ask an adult to make a horizontal cut with a stanley knife a little more than halfway up the bottle.

3

The rectangular shaped bottle must be cut in half, so that you can use the bottom half. Using scissors, cut the bottle in half and then cut all but 5 cm off one of its wider sides.

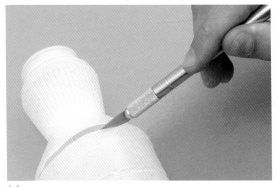

4

For the chimney, take a soft drink bottle that has a nicely shaped neck, and cut the bottle below it. Make sure you ask an adult for help.

5

Now make several vertical cuts below the neck of the bottle, so that you can fold it more easily when you insert this piece into the body of the locomotive.

7

Place the rectangular bottle on the bottom of the cardboard box which you have just prepared, and cut the bottom of the cardboard box a little wider than the shape of the rectangular bottle.

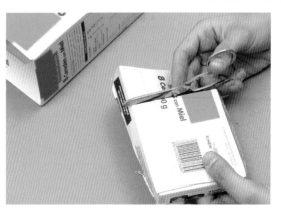

6

Now, take the thin cardboard box and cut the bottom off it. Using scissors, cut the box about 4 cm from the bottom edge.

8

Using adhesive tape, stick a 4 cm strip of cardboard onto the open part of the base of the cardboard box. By doing this, you are going to form a rectangle with four sides, which will fit onto the rectangular plastic bottle.

9

Mark the part of the bottle that you will attach to the carton. Ask an adult to help you cut it with a stanley knife.

You can ask an adult to make all of the holes, so that you can keep working.

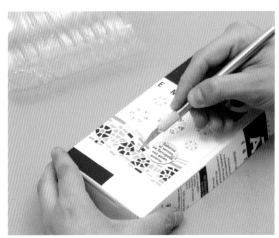

10

You will now begin assembling the central body of the locomotive by mounting the water bottle half onto the carton. Mark the same spots on the Tetra Brick carton. Ask an adult to cut the spots that you have just marked. The cut must be small, so that only the prongs of the paper fastener fit through it.

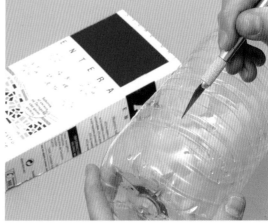

Locomotive

11

Now mount the piece of the water bottle onto the Tetra Brick that you have cut, and secure both parts together by placing two paper fasteners in the places you have pre-cut.

The paper fasteners can work in two ways. If you insert them in a round hole, they turn easily. If you want them to stay firmly fixed, insert them in a hole that has the shape of a straight cut.

12

Insert the paper fasteners at the bottom of the locomotive. These paper fasteners are made of two parts. The front part has two prongs that will go through the plastic or carton that you want to secure in place. The other part is a small metal washer that is placed on the prongs once they have gone through the object that you want to secure in place. Once you have placed this round washer on the prongs, open the prongs to lock the washer in place.

13

Ask an adult to help you cut holes in two water bottle lids. A small cut must be made in the middle of each lid, so that you can insert a paper fastener.

If you have to make a mark on plastic or metal, use permanent markers. But be careful – if you stain your clothes with the markers, it might not come out!

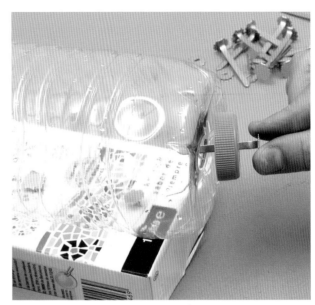

14

At the bottom of the bottle you will find a spot in the middle that is slightly hollowed out. Make a hole in this spot, insert a paper fastener and attach the water bottle lid in place.

15

Once you have secured these pieces together, you will need to make two incisions or cuts with the stanley knife on top of the cylinder. The first cut must be small, in the middle of the cylindrical bottle. Attach the other water bottle lid using a paper fastener in this spot. The other incision or cut must be made at the top part of the cylinder, very close to the front end of the locomotive. This incision must have two cuts in the shape of a cross, so that you can insert the chimney.

Observe locomotives that are in books or magazines, so that you get an idea of what elements you can add. When you see a new element that you might be able to add to your locomotive, study its shape and try to find a similar object at home that you can use.

Locomotive

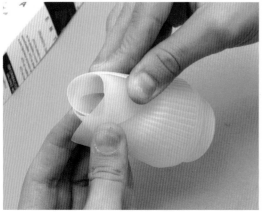

16

You will make the chimney using the neck of the soft drink bottle that you cut off earlier. To do this, fold the bottom of the neck, which is the thicker part. Because of the vertical cuts that you made with scissors, when you fold the neck you will be able to reduce its thickness.

17

Insert the chimney in the cross-shaped cuts that you have made. Once you have inserted half of the chimney or its narrowest section, turn it slightly, so that the section inside the plastic bottle opens correctly and stays locked in place.

So that the wheels spin correctly, do not tighten the paper fasteners very much. Leave a little space between the prongs and their washer.

18

Using a stanley knife or a paper puncher, you must make four holes at the bottom of both sides of the locomotive Tetra Brick carton. You will use these holes to attach the wheels, so they must be the same on all sides.

19

Ask an adult to make holes, using a gimlet, in the middle of the four lids taken from the jelly or vegetable jars. These holes must be made exactly in the centre of the lids, so that the locomotive does not look tilted.

20

Place the wheels in these holes by inserting a paper fastener through both the wheel and the carton. From the inside of the carton, then place the washer on the fastener and open the prongs. Work carefully because the hole in the wheel is very sharp.

21

Using scissors, cut a little more into the side of the rectangular plastic bottle where you have cut off all but 5 cm. You must cut both sides of this small piece, so that you can fold it down.

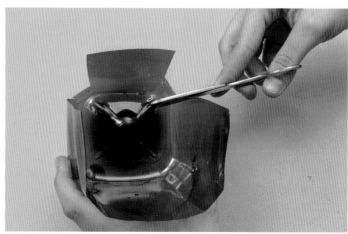

The blades of the scissors at the tip, have less force than further down. If you want to cut a thick material, open up the scissors more and try to cut using the inside part of the scissors.

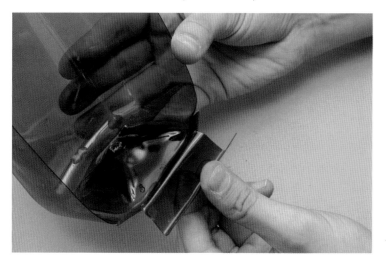

22

Fold down the piece that you have just cut. Then, in the middle of the piece, make a fold outwards.

Locomotive

23

Your adult helper will have to use the gimlet to make a hole in the middle of the bottle. In this hole, you will insert a paper fastener through the bottom of the bottle and the carton, which acts as the base of the locomotive.

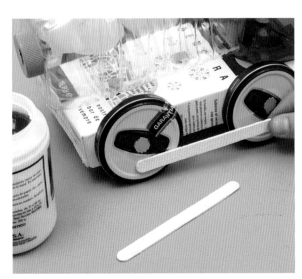

24

Next, take two clean ice-cream sticks and glue them to the wheels using white glue. If they do not stick correctly, you can try to attach them to the paper fasteners that secure the wheels in place.

25

Now you can begin painting the locomotive. Use acrylic paint because plastic does not take watercolours. Paint the body of the locomotive using a bright green colour.

26

Paint the chimney using two colours – black on the bottom and red on the top.

27

Also paint the base of the locomotive black, which is the Tetra Brick carton and the engineer's cabin. Take advantage of the transparent blue colour that the rectangular water bottle has and leave a space on it unpainted for the windows.

28

Using the colour red, paint the ice-cream sticks, the top of the engineer's cabin and the water bottle lids that are mounted at the front and on top of the locomotive.

30

Finally, draw a few details on the locomotive using a gold marker. Wait until the paint is dry to draw them. You can draw the spokes on the wheels, the door handle for the engineer's cabin, or whatever you prefer.

29

Colour the wheels using a black permanent marker.

Locomotive

31
Here is how our locomotive
has turned out after all of
the work we have done.
Doesn't it look nice?